I VOTED

Making a Choice Makes a Difference

MARK SHULMAN

Illustrated by
SERGE BLOCH

NEAL PORTER BOOKS
HOLIDAY HOUSE / NEW YORK

Neal Porter Books

Text copyright © 2020 by Mark Shulman

Illustrations copyright © 2020 by Serge Bloch

All Rights Reserved

HOLIDAY HOUSE is registered in the U.S. Patent and Trademark Office.

Printed and bound in October 2019 at Toppan Leefung, DongGuan City, China.

The art for this book was created by hand and computer, with pleasure, hope, and a little bit of ink.

Book design by Jennifer Browne

www.holidayhouse.com

First Edition

2   4   8   6   8   10   9   7   5   3   1

Library of Congress Cataloging-in-Publication Data

Names: Shulman, Mark, 1962– author. | Bloch, Serge illustrator.

Title: I voted : making a choice makes a difference / Mark Shulman ;

illustrated by Serge Bloch.

Description: First Edition. | New York : Holiday House, [2020] | "Neal Porter Books."

Identifiers: LCCN 2019010713 | ISBN 9780823445615 (Hardcover)

Subjects: LCSH: Voting—United States—Juvenile literature. |

Elections—United States—Juvenile literature.

Classification: LCC JK1978 .S348 2020 | DDC 324.6—dc23

LC record available at https://lccn.loc.gov/2019010713

For Barbara and Bill,
and everyone who works to get out the vote.
See you on election day!
—M.S.

For my father, in remembrance of the days
when he took me to the polling station as a child.
With thanks to Sheina and Blandine.
—S.B.

Which do you like better?

Apples or oranges?

Markers or crayons?

Trampolines or swimming pools?

Some choices are easy to make:
Ice cream or onions?

Some choices are harder:
Ice cream or cupcakes?

Any time you choose one thing instead of another,
you can say that you voted for it.

When you're the only one voting . . .

you tend to get what you want.

But people usually vote together.

Imagine you're choosing a classroom pet.

Everyone will be voting.

And the pet you'll all get

is the pet that most people vote for.

Even if it isn't the one you wanted.

So if you want your choice to win,
here's what you can do before everyone votes.

You can let people know which choice you want.

You can work with the people who want the same thing.

You can talk to the people who want something different.

Maybe you will change their mind.

Maybe they will change yours.

Then when it's time to vote, you vote. It's simple.

Sometimes everyone knows what you chose.

Sometimes it's a secret.

But everyone's vote must get counted.

And the winner is . . . whatever got the most votes.

Maybe your side will win.

And maybe your side will not . . .

But if you don't vote, you don't get to choose.

And your vote might be the one that makes the difference.

Win or lose, when everyone follows the rules, voting is fair for everyone.

It's the same when grown-ups vote.

Grown-ups vote for the people who help run our towns,

our cities, our states, and our country.

They could be mayors, governors, representatives, senators,

or even the president of the United States.

These people pass laws that can change the way we live.

So we have to choose our leaders carefully.
Because different leaders want different things.

Some will do things you really, really like.

Some will do things you really, really don't.

That's why it's important to choose the leaders we want.

So we vote.

We vote for candidates.
A candidate is someone asking for your vote.

How do you know which candidate will make the best choices?

You listen.

You read.

You talk to the people you trust.

Sometimes you can even ask the candidates yourself.

When Election Day finally comes,
everyone goes to the nearest voting place.

Once you've had your 18th birthday,
and your name is added to the list of voters, you can vote, too.

At every voting place, everyone stands in line.

Everyone finds their name on the voter list.

Everyone votes for a candidate.

And someone wins.

If you're old enough, it's important to vote.

If you're not old enough, you know what to do.

Listen. Read. Talk. Ask.

And tell someone who's old enough . . .

to bring you along on Election Day.

When the voting is done, you might get a sticker.

And that sticker will say:

I VOTED.

FIVE EASY STEPS FOR VOTING

1. Be 18 or older.
2. Be a U.S. citizen.
3. Be able to prove where you live in the U.S.
4. Register to vote in your community.
5. Vote every time there is an opportunity.

ONE EASY STEP FOR KIDS

Make sure the adults around you vote on <u>every</u> Election Day . . . if they can!

HOW OUR GOVERNMENT WORKS

We vote for elected officials at the national, state, and local level.

NATIONAL GOVERNMENT

The U.S. government has three main parts, or branches. They are the Executive Branch, the Legislative Branch, and the Judicial Branch.

The Executive Branch includes the president of the United States and those who work directly for the president. Presidential elections are held every four years, and presidents may serve no more than two terms in office. The president lives and works in the White House in our nation's capital, Washington, DC.

The Legislative Branch is also known as Congress. They make and vote on laws that are important to our country. Congress meets in the Capitol Building in Washington, DC. Congress is divided into two chambers: the Senate, and the House of Representatives.

The Senate has 100 members, because each of our 50 states sends two members. Each senator serves for a term of six years, and can be re-elected after that. In the Senate, every state gets an equal vote.

The House of Representatives is a much larger group, 435 members in all. Here, states with larger populations have more members, and get more votes. For instance, Wyoming, which has a very small population, has one representative, while California, which has a very large population, has 53 members. Each representative serves for a two-year term and can be re-elected.

The Judicial Branch consists of judges who help decide if laws are fair, and if people have broken the law. They are charged with upholding the U.S. Constitution. The highest court in the land is the U.S. Supreme Court, which has nine members, including a Chief Justice. Members serve for life and are nominated by the president and confirmed by the U.S. Senate.

The U.S. has two main political parties, the Democratic Party and the Republican Party. Most people register to vote as a Republican, Democrat, or as an Independent, which means you do not belong to either of the two main parties.

STATE GOVERNMENT

Each of our 50 states has a government that mirrors our national government. Each state is led by a governor who, like the president, is the chief executive. Governors are normally elected every four years, and most can be re-elected. Each state also has its own legislative body (like the U.S. Congress) with two houses, or chambers, except for Nebraska, which has only one. State senators and representatives serve for either two or four years. And each state also has its own judicial branch, with judges who uphold the laws in each state.

LOCAL GOVERNMENT

Closer to home, your town or city also has a government. The executive in charge is the mayor. A mayor usually serves for four years. The legislators who work with the mayor are generally called the council. There are many other elected officials where you live—these may include judges, sheriffs, school board representatives, or even the dogcatcher. To find out more, visit the web site of your local government.

YOU CAN START NOW

If you're under the age of 18, remind your family to vote. Every election counts, not just the biggest ones.

There may be opportunities for you to vote in school or in other areas of your life. Maybe you will get to vote for a class pet, as in the book you've just read. You might vote for Class President, or for Student Council. This is very good training for when you're 18 and allowed to vote as a U.S. citizen.

Remember, every time you make a choice, you can say, "I voted."

FIND OUT MORE

BOOKS:

Worth, Bonnie. *One Vote, Two Votes, I Vote, You Vote* (Cat in the Hat's Learning Library). New York: Random House, 2016.

Roosevelt, Eleanor and Markel, Michelle, illustrated by Grace Lin. *When You Grow Up to Vote: How Our Government Works for You*. New York: Roaring Book Press, 2018.

Shamir, Ruby, illustrated by Matt Faulkner. *What's the Big Deal about Elections*. New York: Philomel Books, 2018.

Eggers, Dave, illustrated by Shawn Harris. *What Can a Citizen Do?* San Francisco: Chronicle Books, 2018.

ONLINE:

US Govt: Voting info and games with Ben Franklin
http://bensguide.gpo.gov/9-12/election/

PBS Kids: Videos, trading cards, projects, and more
https://pbskids.org/youchoose

PBS Kids: Presley explains voting to kids
http://safeyoutube.net/w/M38g

Schoolhouse Rock: Three Ring Government
http://safeyoutube.net/w/UbUc

Schoolhouse Rock: I'm Just a Bill
http://safeyoutube.net/w/538g